The Story of

Toys

Monica Hughes

www.raintreepublishers.co.uk
Visit our website to find out more information about **Raintree** books.

To order:
☎ Phone 44 (0) 1865 888112
📄 Send a fax to 44 (0) 1865 314091
💻 Visit the Raintree Bookshop at **www.raintreepublishers.co.uk** to browse our catalogue and order online.

First published in Great Britain by Raintree, Halley Court, Jordan Hill, Oxford OX2 8EJ, part of Pearson Education. Raintree is a registered trademark of Pearson Education Ltd.

© Pearson Education Ltd 2008
The moral right of the proprietor has been asserted.

Editorial: Sian Smith
Design: Kimberley R. Miracle, Big Top and Joanna Hinton-Malivoire
Picture research: Ruth Blair
Production: Duncan Gilbert
Illustrated by Beehive Illustration
Originated by Dot Gradations

Printed and bound in China by Leo Paper Group

ISBN 978 1 4062 1005 7 (hardback)
ISBN 978 1 4062 1015 6 (paperback)

12 11 10 09
10 9 8 7 6 5 4 3 2

British Library Cataloguing in Publication Data
Hughes, Monica
 The story of toys
 1. Toys - History - Juvenile literature 2. Toys - Juvenile literature
 I. Title

688.7'2'09

Acknowledgments
The publishers would like to thank the following for permission to reproduce photographs: ©Alamy p.18 (Orhan Çam); ©Corbis p.6, 13, 5 (Danilo Calilung), 10 (Ray Stubblebine, Hasbro, Handout, Reuters); ©Getty Images pp.7, 9, 19 (AFP), 15 (Dorling Kindersley), 8, 14, 16 (Hulton Archive), 8, 11(News), 9 (Time & Life Pictures), 12 (Roger Voillet); ©istockphoto.com p.4; ©Pearson Education Ltd pp. 5, 12, 13, 17 (Tudor Photography); © Reed International Books Australia Pty Ltd p.4 (Mario Borg)

Cover photograph reproduced with permission of ©Getty Images (Hulton Archive)

Disclaimer
All the Internet addresses (URLs) given in this book were valid at the time of going to press. However, due to the dynamic nature of the Internet, some addresses may have changed, or sites may have changed or ceased to exist since publication. While the author and publisher regret any inconvenience this may cause readers, no responsibility for any such changes can be accepted by either the author or the publisher.

Contents

Some words are printed in bold, **like this**. You can find out what they mean in the glossary.

Old or new?

How can you tell which bear is old and which bear is new?

When something is **new** it has only just been made. When something is **old** it was made a long time ago. It is sometimes difficult to tell if a toy is new or old, but there are things we can look for that help us to find out.

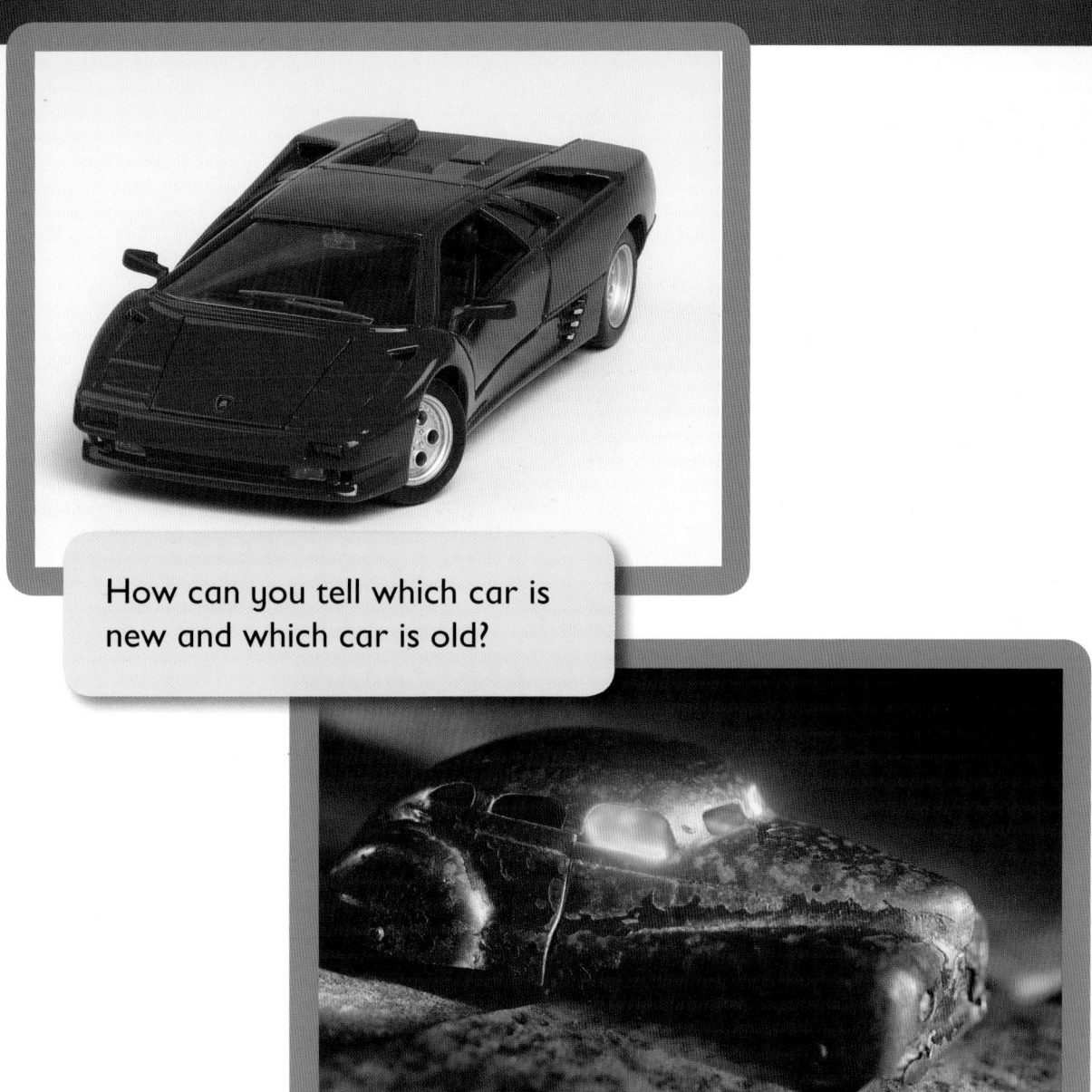

How can you tell which car is new and which car is old?

New toys have usually not been played with very much. They might look clean or shiny. Old toys have usually been played with a lot. Some might be a bit dirty or scruffy. They might be broken. Metal toys can go rusty. A toy that looks rusty might be old.

Old toys

Your grandparents might have had a toy like this. Pushing a button makes the robot walk and make noises.

Children have always loved playing with toys. Your parents, or the people who look after you, had toys when they were children. These toys are **old** today. Your grandparents had toys when they were young. These toys are even older today.

This is a space hopper that your grandparents might have had. You can see **new** space hoppers in toy shops today.

Some older toys were **similar** to toys we have today. Some older toys were different. In this book we will look at old toys that your parents and grandparents might have had. We will **compare** these with toys today to see how they are similar and how they are different.

Dolls then and now

These are dolls your parents might have had.

You can see this new doll in shops today.

Long ago, dolls were often made to look like babies or small children. Dolls like this are still made today, but many are more **realistic**. This means that they look or act more like the real thing. Your parents might have had a doll that could cry. Today dolls can cry, talk, sneeze, smile, eat, drink, and get hiccups.

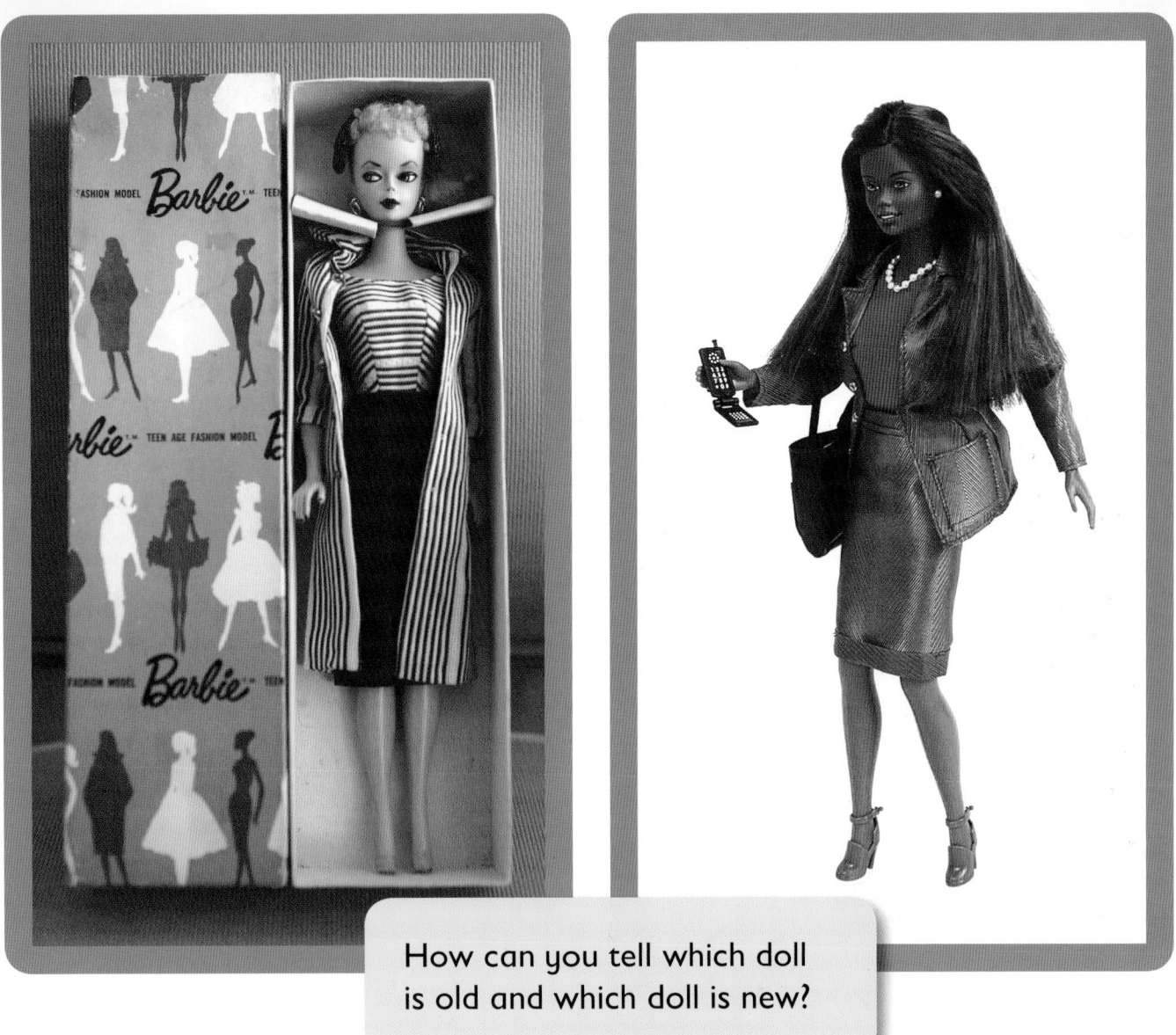

How can you tell which doll is old and which doll is new?

Your parents and grandparents might also have had dolls that looked like grown-ups. They came with extra things such as sunglasses and bags. These are called **accessories**.

We have dolls like this today, but they often come with more accessories. The clothes that dolls wear today might look different, too.

Action figures then and now

Your parents and your grandparents might have had an Action Man.

One of the most **popular** action figures when your grandparents were young was Action Man. These toys were made of plastic and could be dressed up in different clothes. We still have Action Man toys like this today.

Doctor Who figures today.

Most action figures today are made to look like characters from films or television programmes. Your parents might have had figures like this, too. Looking at which characters they show can give you clues about whether the toys are **new** or **old**.

Building things then and now

Meccano today.

A Meccano set that your grandparents might have had.

A favourite building toy when your grandparents were young was Meccano. It was sets of metal bars, with nuts and bolts to fix them together. You could make moving models of things, such as cars and cranes. Later these bars were made of plastic, too. We still have Meccano like this today.

Lego today.

One of the most **popular** building toys when
your parents were young was Lego. You can still
get Lego today and it is almost the same as it
was then. Today though, Lego figures come with
all kinds of different faces. The faces of old Lego
figures only had two eyes and a smiling mouth.

Toy trains then and now

Your grandparents could have had a train set like this. The train moves on electric tracks.

Different types of toy train can move in different ways. Some are pulled or pushed along. Some are wound up with a key. Other toy trains use **electricity** to make them move.

There were all these kinds of toy train when your grandparents and parents were children, and you can find **new** toys like this today.

A toy train today.

Toy trains are often made to look like real trains at the time. So the **design** of these toys can help us to work out if a train is new or **old**. If a toy train looks like a train you might travel on today, it is more likely to be a new toy.

Toy cars then and now

Your parents might have had a toy like this. Pushing the cars made them loop around the track.

We have toy cars today that can be pushed along. There were toy cars like this when your parents and your grandparents were young, too. They might also have had racing cars that moved around **electric** tracks.

We have toys like this today, but we also have racing cars that can be linked to computers and the Internet.

A remote controlled car today.

When your parents were young, they might have had a **remote controlled** car. The first remote controlled cars used batteries and had a wire that joined the car to the remote control. Later toy cars could work without the wire.

Today most remote controlled cars still use batteries, but some can use water and sunlight to make them work.

New types of toy today

Computers today can be very small.

Today we have many different types of computers. Some computers are just for playing games on. Your parents might have had a computer when they were children, but it would have been very different to computers today. Your grandparents wouldn't have had a computer at all when they were young.

Can you tell what game these people are playing?

Computer games are changing all the time. Many games are becoming more **realistic**. This means that they make us feel as if we are really there, in the game.

Do the adults that you know still have any of their **old** toys? Try to find out about how their toys were different from **new** toys today.

Teachers' guide

Because reading ability varies so widely in Year 1, we suggest this book is used in the following way. Read the book through as a whole class activity. Then do the following activities, using the book as a resource at each point, as indicated. The activities could also be done with a variety of images of toys from various time periods. This will allow you to cover the QCA guidelines as fully as possible with as many children as possible.

ACTIVITY 1

- Talk about the various ways you could describe a toy: it's colour, how it feels to touch, is it old or new. Choose any picture in the book. Ask someone to describe it as carefully as possible. Repeat this two or three times until you feel the class is confident with this.

ACTIVITY 2

- Explain that all through history, children have had toys. They have, their parents or carers have, their grandparents have, and their grandparents' grandparents' grandparents, etc. Their toys are newer than their parents' toys, and their parents' toys are newer than their grandparents' toys. Discuss how you can tell if a toy is old or new (What is it made from? Does it look new or as if it has been played with a lot?) Choose three pictures in the book that you could label 'old', 'newer' and 'newest'.

ACTIVITY 3

- Compare two similar toys from different points in the past. Brainstorm a list of their similarities and differences. You could do this with the teddies and cars on pages 4 and 5. Once you have done this you could move onto the trains on pages 14 and 15, where the children have to work harder to find the trains. This can lead to a discussion of what else they would like to see in a modern train set to make comparisons with the older photo.

ACTIVITY 4

- If possible, ask a parent/carer/classroom assistant to come in and talk about one of their toys (with the toy). Discuss beforehand what questions they might like to ask (Did you have many toys? Why was this your favourite?). If possible, take a photo of the visitor and her/his toy and make a display of 'XX and his/her toy', which gives the answers to the questions they asked in speech bubbles around the photo.

ACTIVITY 5

- QCA suggest a visit to a toy museum, see 'Possible visit' below. Even if a visit is not possible, you need to discuss museums (maybe using downloaded images from various websites). Discuss how they are classified: some museums classify by date, some by type, some by type and date. Stress that the most important thing in a good museum is clear and careful labels, so the visitors can find out as much as possible about the exhibits.

ACTIVITY 6

- Borrow as many toys as possible from the children, their families, staff, etc. to create a toy museum. Discuss how to arrange them: by date oldest to newest? By type of object (cuddly toy/trains/cars/puzzles, etc).. If borrowing is difficult, you could build up a photo museum instead: get photos of as many toys belonging to children, their families, people at the school etc as possible and display these alongside other images you have found. This will enable you to talk about the fact that sometimes you know more about one object in a museum than another: so in this case, sometimes you know the owner of a toy and sometimes not.

Possible visit

QCA suggest a toy museum visit. You can find various toy museums listed online if you search on Toy museum UK with the 'UK only' search button. However, most local museums, while not being specialist toy museums, will have a selection of toys on display and may even provide a selection on loan to schools. Contact your local museum to find out what they provide.

Find out more

Books

Changes: Toys and Games, Liz Gogerly
(Hodder Wayland, 2004)

Life in the Past: Victorian Toys, Mandy Ross
(Heinemann Library, 2004)

Then and Now: Having Fun, Vicki Yates
(Heinemann Library, 2008)

Ways Into History: Toys and Games, Sally Hewitt
(Franklin Watts, 2004)

What Was it Like in the Past? Toys, Kamini Khanduri
(Heinemann Library, 2002)

Websites

**www.bbc.co.uk/schools/victorians/standard/play/learning/
toys/index.shtml**
Find out about toys children might have played with about one
hundered years ago.

www.museumofchildhood.org.uk
This museum in London has displays about toys and childhood.

Glossary

accessories extra things that come with a toy, such as sunglasses, bikes, and hats

compare look at two or more things to see how they are the same and how they are different

design the shape or style of something

electric something that uses electricity to make it work

electricity type of energy used to make machines work

new only just been made

old made a long time ago

popular liked by many people

realistic made to look or act like the real thing

remote controlled controlling something from a distance

similar nearly the same as another thing

Index